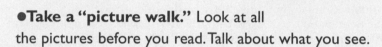

Dear Family,

What's the best way to help your child love reading?

Find good books like this one to share—and read together!

Here are some tips.

●**Take a "picture walk."** Look at all the pictures before you read. Talk about what you see.

●**Take turns.** Read to your child. Ham it up! Use different voices for different characters, and read with feeling! Then listen as your child reads to you, or explains the story in his or her own words.

●**Point out words as you read.** Help your child notice how letters and sounds go together. Point out unusual or difficult words that your child might not know. Talk about those words and what they mean.

●**Ask questions.** Stop to ask questions as you read. For example: "What do you think will happen next?" "How would you feel if that happened to you?"

●**Read every day.** Good stories are worth reading more than once! Read signs, labels, and even cereal boxes with your child. Visit the library to take out more books. And look for other JUST FOR YOU! BOOKS you and your child can share!

The Editors

In loving memory of my mother, Marion C. Black.
And for my cousin Yvonne—
thanks for stirring the memories
—SWB

For **my** Mommy!
With thanks to Aqueel, Aniya, Bria, and LaShawn
—JK

Text copyright © 2004 by Sonia W. Black.
Illustrations copyright © 2004 by Jennifer Kindert.
Produced for Scholastic by COLOR-BRIDGE BOOKS, LLC, Brooklyn, NY
All rights reserved. Published by SCHOLASTIC INC.
JUST FOR YOU! is a trademark of Scholastic Inc.

Library of Congress Cataloging-in-Publication Data

Black, Sonia
    Mommy's bed / by Sonia W. Black ; illustrated by Jennifer Kindert.
        p. cm.—(Just for you! Level 1)
    Summary A boy relates all the things he and his sisters do in their mother's
bed—such as read, tickle, and play—that make it the best place to be.
Includes activity ideas for parents and children.
        ISBN 0-439-56857-9 (pbk.)
        [1. Beds—Fiction. 2. Family life—Fiction. 3. African Americans—
Fiction.] I. Kindert, Jennifer C., ill. II. Title. III. Series.
PZ7.B5294Mo 2004
[E]—dc22   2004042917

10 9   12
Printed in the U.S.A. 40 • First Scholastic Printing, February 2004

Mommy's Bed

by Sonia W. Black

Illustrated by Jennifer Kindert

I have my very own bed.
My sisters have their
own beds, too.

This is our Mommy's bed.
Mommy's bed is the best.

In Mommy's bed
we have lots of fun.
We talk about school
and Mommy's busy day.

We eat
and drink.

We play.

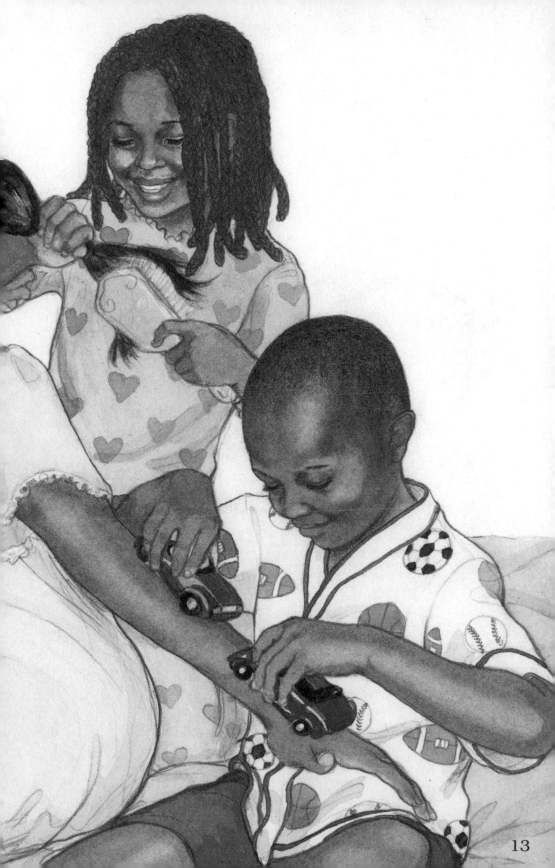

We sing.

We read.

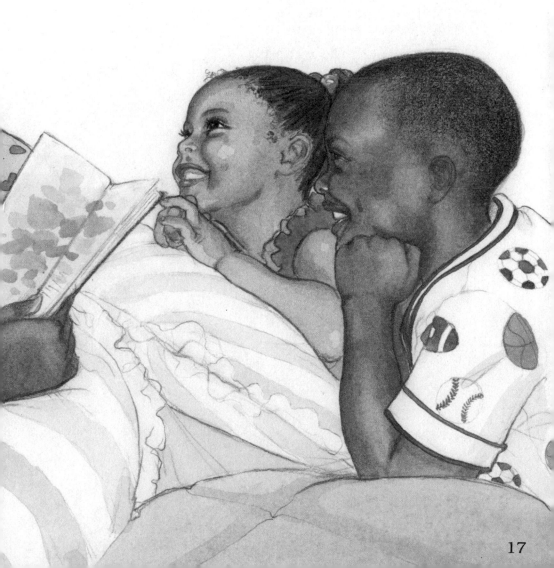

We watch TV.

We tickle.
We laugh.

We cry.

We give hugs and kisses.

Our Mommy's bed
is the best because . . .

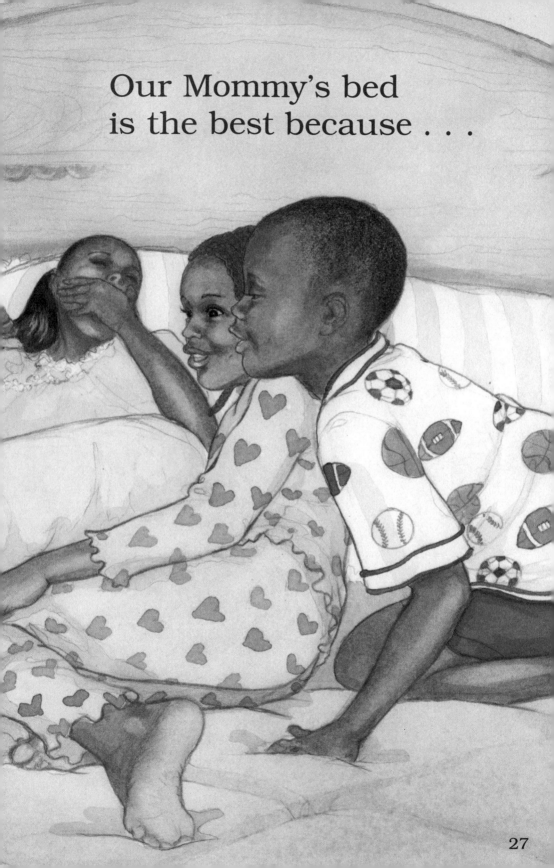

Mommy's bed
is soft
and warm
and cozy,
just like Mommy!

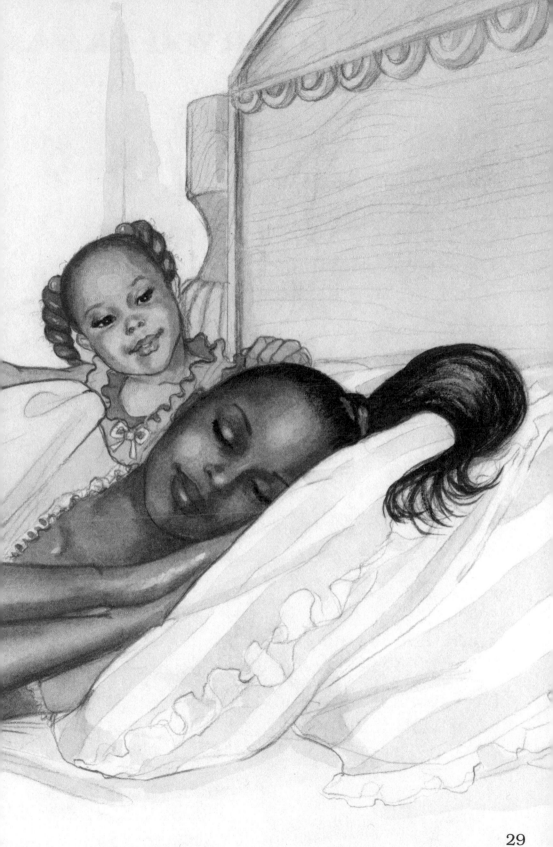

▲▲▲▲▲JUST FOR YOU ▲▲▲▲▲

Here are some fun things for you to do.

It's the Best!

The children say Mommy's bed is the best place to do many things.

They like to **play** there. Where do YOU like to play?

They like to **talk** there. Where do YOU like to talk?

They even like to **eat** there! Where do YOU like to eat?

Think about your home. What is YOUR best place?

Draw a picture to show what YOU like to do there.

It's Cozy, Too!

The children say Mommy's bed is **soft**. What else is soft?

They say it's **warm**. What else is warm?

They say it's **cozy**. What else would YOU say is cozy? Tell why.

▲▲▲▲TOGETHER TIME▲▲▲▲

Make some time to share ideas about the story with your young reader! Here are some activities you can try. There are no right or wrong answers!

Talk About It: Ask your child, "How is our family like the one in this story? How is it different?" What do you do at the end of a busy day? What are your favorite things to do together?

Think About It: Point out the title and the author on the book's cover. Then read aloud "Meet the Author" on page 32. Ask your child, "Why do you think Sonia Black picked this title for her story? If you wrote a story about our family, what title would you use?"

Read It Again: Read the story aloud. Stress words that describe the family's actions, such as *eat, drink, watch, play, read, talk, tickle, laugh,* and *cry*. Help your child by pointing to these words as you read. Together, make reading even more fun by acting out these words, too!

Meet the Author

SONIA W. BLACK says, "This story comes from memories of the happiest times my three sisters and I shared with our mother. Her bedroom was our gathering place. Often when she'd just crawled into bed, tired from a long day's work, we'd all pile in to be with her— talking, laughing; enjoying precious Mommy-time!"

Sonia was born in Kingston, Jamaica. When she was eleven, her family moved to Brooklyn, New York. Her love of writing began there, at PS 9, where she enjoyed creative writing classes with Miss Gibbs, a favorite teacher who read wonderful poetry and short stories aloud. After graduating from Wilmington College in Ohio, Ms. Black went to work for a publishing company and became a children's book editor. Her books for beginning readers include *Hanging Out with Mom, Plenty of Penguins,* and *Home for the Holidays.* She lives in New Jersey with her two lovely daughters, Greyson and Evanne.

Meet the Artist

JENNIFER KINDERT says, "I really got to know the children you see in this story. I had to take many photographs of them to use as a guide when I was ready to draw and paint. Some things you see in my pictures came from photos, but many came from my imagination. I can make up whatever I want to put down on my drawing paper—and so can you! Illustrating a book is hard work. I love what I do, so it is worth every bit of it!"

Jennifer studied at the International Art School in Stockholm, Sweden, where she grew up. She received a Bachelor of Fine Arts degree from the Fashion Institute of Technology in New York City. After working for several years as a graphic designer in New York, she moved to Dallas, Texas. Her first book in the JUST FOR YOU! series, *Hurry Up!*, was published in 2003.